Victory of Words

Poetry Collection

1,100 Poem Challenge Volume 4

Victory of Words Poetry Collection

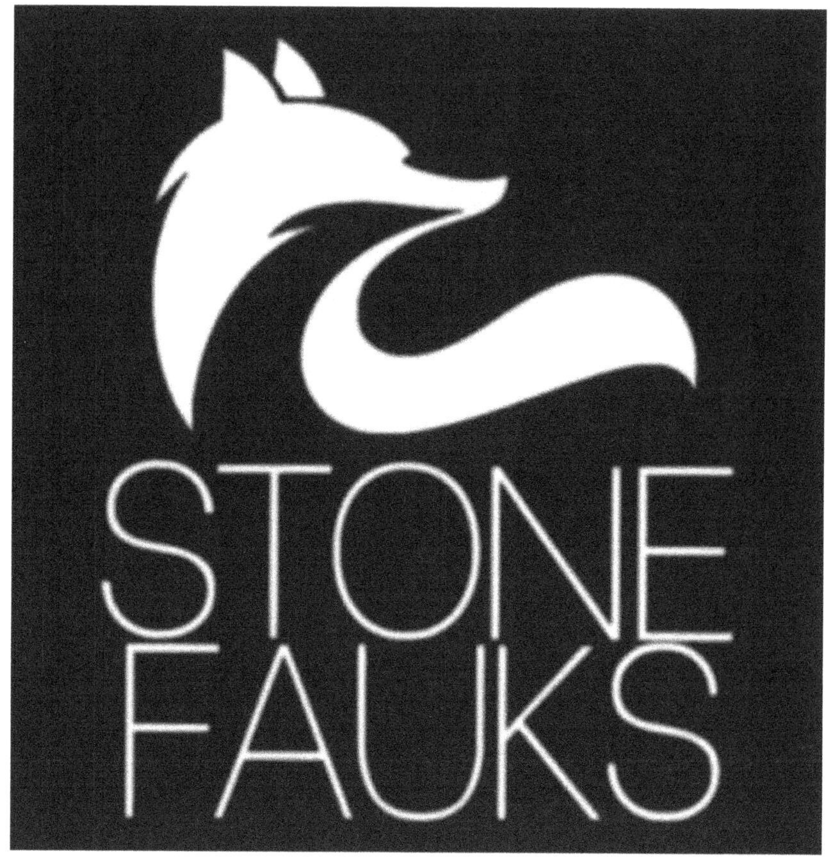
STONE
FAUKS

Preface

When I was in school, the parents had the option to come up to the school to get our report cards or just have the children bring them home. My mother always concerned about my education would leave work early, come to my school, get my report card, and talk to my teachers. One day when I was in grammar school, after she got my grades and saw my reading score was the lowest in the class. I had an F in reading. My mother asked my teacher. What could she do to improve my grades? She didn't leave it to the teacher to do all the work, to teach me, to educate me. She took matters into her own hands. The teacher told her to read with me and have me read to her. After school that day we went to a store and bought some books, I don't remember what store, I don't even remember what books we bought, but I do remember us reading together that day. She would read to me, but most often I would read to her, anytime I mispronounce a word or had trouble with a word she would help me figure it out.

From there I developed a love for reading. I started with comic books and then onto Poetry, because they were short, even though not always easy to understand. Eventually I moved to short stories and novels.

I fell in love with reading so much so that I developed a desire to write. I was more interested in writing poetry because I felt I could express myself freer through poetry, than telling someone else's story.

From fourteen years old to my late thirties. I'd written hundreds of poems, and I had completed my first short story. After a big fight with my wife. I stayed with my mom for a few days, when I went back home, I couldn't find my writings anywhere, my wife said she didn't know where they were. I kept them in one place so I could easily find them. I checked the whole house and never found them. She never confessed to tossing them. I had become overprotective of my work.

I was always nervous about publishing my poetry, I was always self-conscious about people not liking what I wrote. Despite my fears I entered contests and performed my poems on stage. I guess it was because the praise was instantaneous.

I saw a Facebook add for a self-publisher, I discussed it with my girlfriend, she told me to go for it, and she would help anyway she could. I contacted the publisher we discussed prices, and I selected 50 poems, formatted them, and sent them to the publisher.

A few months later I agreed to do an interview with Stu Taylor. I wasn't as nervous as I thought I'd feel. It was quick and exciting.

I continued writing poetry and I've started a few short stories. But I didn't push myself to do anything special. Surfing around Instagram and Threads I saw a few poets had done a poem a day for thirty days challenge. On YouTube I saw an influencer reacting to a young lady's work and he pointed out everything he thought was wrong with her books. I thought about how I had been around longer than her and I'm still unknown.

I decided I had to do something more with my writing I had to publish more.

The thirty-day challenge was good, but I felt that wasn't a good challenge for me. My original goal was to write one thousand poems in a year. After doing the math I realized if I did three poems it would come to 1,095 and I figured I could add five more to make it 1,100.

I started this challenge on September 1, 2024

These books are a collection of poems on various subjects.

This book is the fourth and final book in the four-volume series, each book will contain 275 poems. That will be three poems a day until August 27, 2025, when I will write four poems a day till the end of the month which will give me the 1,100.

Thank you for your interest and support.

Stone Fauks

Tough Skin

Your heart and mind must be calloused
leathery, coarse, and rough, you must have
Alligator skin, thick, hard to penetrate
Wolverine skin, instant healing
Kryptonian skin, invulnerable to all kinds
of weapons
Tougher skin withstands rejection,
backbiting, slander, naysayers, and doubters.
Having tough skin keeps you moving forward
despite the negativity of others
(826)

Acceptance

I've had a hard life, financial struggles,
relationship problems, being jobless,
and being homeless.
I wouldn't change a thing.
A man is defined by the hardships
he overcomes and his growth.
I've learned there are many ways
to earn income and build wealth,
a couple stays together
when each helps the other
through stress and worry.
(827)

Rum Cake

A stroll along the sand
walking hand in hand
Teasing with sweet words
chasing away the birds
We run together into the surf
we dry out lying on the turf
Listening to the radio we sing to each other,
we laugh and play till we're ready for slumber
We scatter the stresses of the week
filling our love and peace to its peak
(828)

Abandonment

Where do I walk
Through the forest preserve
where am I going
To an uncertain future
What is my goal
To obtain success
What am I searching for
True love
What do I find
Unrequited love
Will I find a woman to love
Only God knows
(829)

Manifesting

My vision board hung on my bedroom wall,
A stack of books with my pseudonym
A three-bedroom house
A 97 Jaguar xj8
And various cruises and trips
Things started to happen
I began to write and study writing everyday
I found a house that was in my budget
Still looking for the car
But I take trips every year
(830)

Robbing Your Goals

You're wasting your goals
by not deferring your gratification.
You're stealing from your future
by using your resources now.
You're robbing your future
by not being disciplined today.
(831)

Fuck It

Life doesn't get easier.
We just get to the point when
we say, "FUCK IT!"
and mean it.
We become emotionally
Calloused to mistreatment
and stop being kind
We stop making excuses
for bad behavior
and accept they want to hurt us
and say, "FUCK IT."
(832)

Welcome to My World

"I wish I was as strong as you."
"It's not easy to do."
"You never have any strife."
"Being strong is a way of life."
"I'm afraid to say what I feel."
"When you get fed-up, you will."
"I'm worried they'll hate me."
"Stop people pleasing and you'll be free."
"I work hard but it's not appreciated."
"No appreciation for work is to be accepted."
"I wish I was as strong as you."
"It's not easy to do."
"Why is speaking up so hard."
"Because your emotions are on guard."
(833)

Wake Up Call

Sunlight through my window
wakes me from my slumber
A cool breeze and singing birds
wakes my body and mind
My wife walks in, climbs in the bed,
kisses my lips and says, “It's time to get up.”
“I'm up.” I mumble.
“I wasn't talking to you.”
She winks and kisses my chest.

(834)

Butterflies

At a loss for words
Like butterflies float away
Drifting on the breeze
(835)

The Kit

Tools of a writer
Pen, paper, creativity
Nature and quiet
(836)

Achievements

To be stronger, learn to enjoy
lifting heavy weights
To lose weight get used
to feeling hungry
To become successful,
get in the habit of working
on your plans
when you don't feel like it
For a happy relationship
discuss the negative
To become smarter,
get comfortable studying
To have a happy life
find solutions to hardships

(837)

The Thief in Me

Whether it was to gain wealth
Whether it was to meet a need
It was all selfish
I didn't think of how the other person
would feel
I only thought about what I wanted
Whether it was money, time, or love
I took what I wanted
I wasn't compassionate about
the other person's needs or wants
as long as I got mine
I am a dishonest person
I have been for a long time
I have debts to pay

(838)

Crisis

A broken heart, how will I survive
A lost job, how will I survive
Mom passed, how will I survive
Tears every day, how will I survive
(839)

Perception

People are not who you want them to be
Most people are not who you think they are
Until you spend time with them,
you'll never know their heart
(840)

Flowers

Sunflowers for your character
Violets for your beauty
Lilacs for your scent
Roses for your love
Tulips for your kiss
(841)

Metals

Iron for your confidence
Steel for your strength
Tin for your resilience
Gold for your wealth
Zinc for your power
(842)

Me Time

He needed silence but received conversation
He wanted peace but was given confusion
He felt trapped, confined, boxed in
He wanted to plug his ears but that would be rude
He had to endure the commotion
till he arrived home so he could be alone
Twenty hours of being surrounded by extroverts
burned his brain
No one noticed the tears rolling down his face
No one noticed his agony
(843)

Trust

Harry tried not to crush his daughter's hand. He hoped she didn't feel his hand shaking. He had to be strong for her; he had to be tough and protect her.

This was a new neighborhood in a new city. A city with a reputation for violence.

Suzy gripped her dad's hand as they walked the dark street her vision blurry, her body was hot and cold, her steps were clumsy. She wondered. How was daddy so confident, so fearless?

(844)

Vision

Can you see the future
Can you see what is on the horizon
Can you touch it, taste it, feel it
Do you dream about it
Are you excited to have it
Do you want it or is it your desire
Does it flood your mind night and day
Is your life empty without it
Then do it

(845)

The Cause of Diseases

CDC or the lack of the CDC panel
is the cause of dis-ease
Dis-ease of health
Dis-ease of wealth
Dis-ease of trust
Politicians are more interested in control
than they are in health
They want to make sure their bank accounts
are healthy while the country dies around them
(846)

Man of Action

An idea is a want
A dream is wishful thinking
A plan is hope
Only action will make it real
Only movement will produce it
Only consistent action will give it life
(847)

RPGS

Red hair
Pink nails
Gray dress
Scarlet shoes
(848)

Restless

Body irritated
I can't sit still
Thoughts aimless
Mind exhausted
Can't find comfort
Back hurts
Restless legs
Shoes tight,
Feet swelling
No position eases
my restlessness
(849)

Whirlwind

We get information from everyone, around us bad, and
good. Especially when we're going through a crisis, we
look for answers and direction
There is a whirlwind of information floating in the world,
we can blame others for giving wrong advice,
but we have to take responsibility for our actions
We are flawed people asking for help from other
flawed people
We can listen to advice from others, but we have to
decide if that is the type of person we want to be.
I watched a video where a man was blaming another
man for telling him to sleep with a lot of women, and
how it messed up his life. If he took accountability for his
own actions, he should've asked himself, if he wanted to
be a womanizer, did he want that kind of reputation.

A lot of times we will follow wrong advice knowing it's wrong so we can blame our wickedness on others instead of being responsible and accountable.

It's easy to point your finger at other people and say they
told you to do something, but it is your responsibility
to make the right decision.

(850)

Firefly

Sitting on the back porch watching the sunset
The warm summer breeze glides past me
Stars slowly appear
Dim yellow lights flicker near the ground
Soon my backyard is filled with tiny twinkling lights
I'm mesmerized by the show
my mind wanders as the fireflies, dance

(851)

The Bones of My Enemies

My throne was built from the bones of my enemies
My crown was forged from their fingers
My breastplate was formed from their shattered skulls
I became my hero
I was my motivator
I was my problem solver
My Enemies laughed and mocked while I cried
They ridiculed my pain
Lift my head because they tried to shame me
My victories made their bones brake
My achievements caused them to bleed
My successes destroyed them

(852)

Hindrances

First laziness, wanting to stop just because
it seems hard
Second doubts, not trusting your skills
Third Fear, people won't like my product
Fourth 2nd level of laziness, this is taking too long,
or that's enough, or good enough
Fifth 2nd level doubt, I'm not good enough to do this
Sixth 2nd level fear, no one is gonna support me
Seventh distractions, Oh shit I almost forgot to work on
my project today.
I'll do extra work on it tomorrow

(853)

Backpack in the Corner

My dusty slack backpack is in the bedroom corner
The places we've traveled to, the beach, the park,
work, Chesapeake, Dugway, Rawlings
The things you've carried, lunch, snacks, notebook,
pens, clothes, toothbrush
You've been tossed, kicked, carried, pulled
Now you're resting, waiting for our next adventure
(854)

Random Bits of Information

My mind is filled with random bits of information
Some are useful, and some a waste brain cells
Old jokes, bad choices, the first time I felt love,
the time my heart was broken
The day my daughter was born,
the day I lied to a friend
Random bits of information roam through
my mind

(855)

Tower

Working to build a tower of skill
a monument to talent
Old structures have begun to crumble
and need to be rebuilt
Studying deeply
to make the foundation strong
Practicing often to reinforce the base
The tower slowly rises

(856)

Free Rider

He's looking for a handout
for any freebies he can grab
Quick and easy income to spend
he doesn't care about saving
He only wants what he can get now
Tomorrow is too far away,
today is all that matters
and any available free rides

(857)

The Best

For Marcus, daily training was a way of life
Not only was it a great exercise
but he also improved his skill
He started training to beat his opponents
Now he knew he could beat them
he just improved himself for fun
Everyone said he was the best,
but he understood that
with plenty of practice anyone
could be better.

(858)

Blurred Vision

The work was too hard
The dream faded
The work was boring
The goal waned
The plan took too long
The plan dried up
It's easier to work on someone else's
dream than it is to work on mine.
The vision I had for my future
(859)

Am I Finished

Am I done or do I have more to say
This challenge is now challenging
Can I go to another level
or is this where I end
Have I reached the end of my creativity
or is this a wall I must break through
Is this the next step in my evolution
or is this where I end

(860)

Monument

Every artist has their signature, I can't see mine
Am I a poet, philosopher, motivator,
a combination, or something different?
Who am I, what do I do, where do I go
Using emotional clay shape myself
(861)

Starlight

The sun has set
The Moon has risen
Starlight fills the sky
I think of us and the times we shared
A glint of light catches my eye
I'm drawn to the dark spot
I remember my hunt for you
And my confession of my love
A shooting star crosses my sight,
and I think of how I chased after you
The starlit sky is full of memories of us.

(862)

Chaff

Pulling, tugging, and ripping off the outer layer
Struggling to get to the new flesh underneath
Red, tender, exposed muscle
the cool air burning like fire
The old me lying on the ground
the shell of who I used to be
in a heap at my feet
The past life cast aside, shriveled,
and dried blown away with a gust of wind
I must let this new skin take shape
and harden into the new me

(863)

A New Me

I need to build
To shape
To form
To align
I need to make
To mold
To layout
To configure
There is a new me
Bubbling up and boiling over
The new me is here

(864)

Sweetheart

Kind eyes
A cute laugh
A playful kiss
A gentle smile
Some corny jokes
A comforting hug
An opening heart
(865)

Storms

Storms strengthen your psyche
calm cycles are for contemplation
During dark days decisions are made
Calamities create a new life course
(866)

Good Luck Charm

You are my blessing,
my good luck charm
When we hold hands
The sun shines brighter
When we hug
The air is fresher
When we kiss
The world is a better place
When you talk,
I hear my favorite song
your smile makes
my heart beat faster
You are my lucky charm
(867)

Girl of My Dreams

She is my muse
She tells me she cares
She laughs at my corny jokes
She rubs my back and my feet
She understands why I'm quiet
She knows when to motivate me
She discerns if I need gentle or tough love

(868)

Al Fresco

When I was young, we stayed outside,
especially in the summer
We had cookouts, picnics, barbeques,
and sometimes went camping
Outside was life, inside was punishment
if you were called to come in, your day was over.
Now eating outside is remembering my younger days
When we partied with family and played
today no one wants to pick up the mantle
to have cookouts, picnics, or barbeques
So now any outside meal will do

(869)

Low Self

Looking at what I've written over the past 10 months, excepting myself, and the rejection of others
constantly turns up.
It tells me I'm still battling low self-esteem.
I could talk about my esteem issues for hours.
what if instead of battling self-esteem I was actually
on a journey of understanding myself through art
what if in my art I find each piece beautiful
because it builds me

(870)

The Dark Night

Tonight was darker than usual only stars filled the sky

I searched for the moon it was nowhere to be seen

It was like someone forgot to pay the moonlight bill

The power was turned off and it wouldn't come on again until the past-due amount was paid

The stars twinkled trying to fill the void but to no avail

I tracked the heavens for Earth's companion, but he was gone like my dad when he left to buy cigarettes

(871)

Misunderstanding

Cleaning the cafeteria at the end of my day, wipe down the counters and clean the sink, preparing to wipe down the tables and the chairs. A sales associate walks in and says in a soft voice "Eww I'm so wet. Why is this thing so wet. "

I booked my eyes and say excuse me

then she says, "look it's dripping everywhere."

I turned and looked at her and she pointed at the microwave

"I don't know. But I'll clean it up." I think to myself, "man I have to get my head out of the gutter."

(872)

Yes, to Your Love

I said "no," to arguing
I said "yes," to talking
I said "no," to fighting
I said "yes," to hugging
I said "no," to lying
I said "yes," to honesty
I said "no," to cheating
I said "yes," to being faithful
I said "no," to hatred
I said "yes," to loving
I said "no," to being enemies
I said "yes," to being lovers
(873)

Turning Leaves

I turned the leaves of others' hearts seeking
for similarities
I peeked inside ancient minds looking
for something new
I walked for miles in another's shoes
trying to reach a unique understanding
I peered through the eyes of troubled souls
trying to comprehend peace
I've listened to distant voices
trying to hear the unknown
I found that life doesn't change
the only important thing is how we live it.
(874)

Brain Overload

She doesn't love me
She doesn't want me
Bills past due
Late for work
Missed deadlines
Projects delayed
She wants to move
She wants jewels
car broke down
Kids sick
High blood pressure
Sleepless nights

(875)

Shenanigans

dirty tricks
fooling around
funny business
hanky-panky
high jinks
horsing around
monkey business
clowning around
Fun
(876)

Your Voice

I love your enthusiasm
when you're expressing your point
Your voice is so soft and feminine
Your laugh is the sweetest sound
I've heard
delicate and womanly
(877)

Motivation

What is the next step?
I'm tired of learning,
I'm tired of motivation
I'm tired of advice
I need the next step
I need decisions and action
I'm ready for growth
Where do I look
(878)

Storms at Sea

Winds uncontrolled releasing their full fury
Waves as tall as mountains flinging everything
on its surface
Clouds emitting their power
Sea creatures diving deep fleeing the rage above
Seeking the calm below
Sinking into the darkness searching for peace
(879)

Self-Satisfied

I don't like the size of my stomach
but it's smaller than it has been
I don't like how tired my eyes look
but I feel energetic
I don't like how scruffy my beard is
but it's growing nicely
I don't like that I must use a cane to walk
but I can still walk
I see all of my shortcomings,
but I also see my strengths
I am satisfied with myself and the life I have.

(880)

Risking a War to End a War

Leaders fighting leaders, the men you're fighting
are not wimps
They're willing to kill just like he is
There is more than one way to fight an opponent
He destroyed their nukes, they can use other means
to attack.
He thinks it will take them years
to rebuild their nuclear force.
Don't let his ego draw the world into a war.
Trump used bombs to stop a war.
He killed a bunch of people to stop killing people.

(881)

Sweaty Day

Ninety-eight degrees,
a normal summer day
Self-doubt, and fear,
I break out in a cold sweat
Failures flood my mind
as I contemplate the first step
What if I do succeed
can I maintain that quality
Sweat running down my back
fears flood my mind

(882)

Strays

We are all strays,
looking for a place to love
A home, a shelter
A place to protect us
from the dangers of the world.
We may have a roof over our heads,
but we are still in search of comfort and love
We are all strays looking for a place to love

(883)

2025

I failed
I cried
I lost hope
I was afraid
I doubted myself
I lost family
Friends walked away
I bought a cane to help me walk
I celebrated sixty years
I celebrated the grand addition
to a friend's family
I overcame hardships,
and I enjoyed happy days
I survived

(884)

Self Portrait

Bags under my eyes
Crow's feet at my eye
Graying hair
beard white
Strength weakening
Belly sagging
Joints aching
Confidence higher
Outlook on life brighter
Hope building
Days buzzing past
(885)

Midnight Hammer

The Hammer hit three nails on the head
and sealed the door shut
The next few weeks or months will reveal
the consequences of those Hammer strikes
A businessman is fighting a war against a strategist
Only so many bases can be protected
I understand why we are coming to Israel's aid,
but I also know we may have made a bigger war.
Don't let arrogance cause our downfall. A superior
fighting force doesn't mean much to a skilled strategist.

(886)

A Piece of My Heart

I am offering you a piece of my heart,
a part of my love, a corner of my soul
I am offering you a piece of my heart,
a part of my character, a snippet of my spirit
I am offering you a piece of my heart,
a part of my life, I am asking you to take my name

(887)

Mach War

Three facilities were bombed but no people were in these facilities
Iran retaliated by bombing the American base in Doh Ha with the same number of bombs that were used against
them.
I don't want people to die it is good that no one was hurt
or killed
buuuutt it seems kind of sus to me that a base as big
as Doh Ha has that the base was vacant.
Is this a real conflict or something that was drummed up
to draw everyone's attention from something even
bigger

(888)

The Desire of Creativity

Emotional Love is a feeling of creativity
The sexual urge is a desire for creativity
Making love is an act of creation
(889)

Symbolism

Iran didn't want a war
But they wanted to show strength
They didn't want to cowardly surrender
They told America where they were going to bomb
so the base could be cleared
Light munitions were deployed then peace talks began
(890)

Tired

Ninety-degree heat
Siphoning my energy
Sweating through the labor
Discipline through the doubt
Working despite my emotions
Fatigue my companion
(891)

You Know

You know who you are
you know what you do
you know who you are to me
I love your heart.
I love your smile
you're special to me.
you know who you are
you know what you do
you know what you mean to me
you are my light
you are my love.
You are the one for me.

(892)

Summer Night Sounds

Crickets chirping, grasshoppers buzzing,
eighties R and B, children laughing,
Greg and his wife fighting again
Glass breaking, baby crying, sirens wailing,
a dog barking.
Stressed environment, congested living,
pressured habitat
a summer night in the city
the soundtrack of my life

(893)

Display

Sheila walked into the office makeup perfect, her hair neat, her short pencil dress accentuating her figure, stockings making her legs look sleek, and heels matching her handbag.

Harry looked up when she entered.

She smiled at him; she was crushing on him so hard.

She had to get him to fall for him, and so far, nothing was working. He nodded at her and went back to his work.

"Damn, she is sexy." He mumbled to himself. Then he returned his focus on completing his assignment so he could leave an hour early so he could finish the project for his client.

He was attracted to Sheila, but he didn't want to work here forever, he couldn't let her distract him from his financial goal.

(894)

Poems

Poems don't have to be profound
they just need to tug at the heart
Poems don't need to be long,
but they must tell a story
Poems don't need to rhyme
but there should be music
Poems don't have to have symbolism,
but they must have a meaning
Poems don't need flowery words
but there should be beauty
Poems are self-expression
and don't have to be shared with anyone

(895)

Lunch Buddy

Tia and I were going to lunch at the same time. She asked
me did I wanted to eat together. "Yeah, that'd be great."
We laughed and teased each other. She asked if we could
lunch together tomorrow. "Sure, sounds good."
I thought, "Tia you're looking for someone you can eat
lunch with I'm looking for someone I can sleep with.
You're looking for a guy you can eat with I'm looking
for a woman I can eat."

(896)

A Ray of Sunlight in a Thunderstorm

The only ray of sunshine,
the only happiness in my life,
the one thing that gives me peace of mind
in this tsunami that is my life
is spending time
with the woman who despises me.
(897)

Listening

Lying in our bed in the darkened bedroom
The rain pelting against the window
The hard wind blowing
Cars splashing in potholes
Your soft breathing
Our bed creaking as I turn

(898)

Tonight

Fresh air, a warm breeze, strolling through the park
Holding hands, playful kisses, slow jams streaming
Romantic night, keeping things new, a couple young at heart
Tonight is a night of love, a time of intimate fun, tonight we remember being young

(899)

Bratty Girl

All a bratty girl needs
is a good spanking
and a hard pounding
(900)

Becoming The Storm

Malik stood on the shore and watched
the approaching dark clouds.
He held his ground against the force of the wind.
A torrent poured from the clouds wetting his hair,
his clothes, his skin, his bones.
He balled up his fist, he gritted his teeth,
his whole body tensed. A rumble started in his chest,
rose to his throat, and exploded from his mouth.
He screamed about his financial problem,
the fights with his wife and children,
the struggles at his job. Tears mixed with the rain.
He was tired of hurting, of fighting, of struggling.
The storm ended, the sky cleared, the sun shone.
He understood the only way to have peace is to stand strong against the wind, the downpour.
To allow the lightening to explode from his heart.

(901)

Luxury

You have the luxury to weep
I have the burden of strength
You have the luxury of sleep
I have the burden of the day's length
You have the luxury of doubt
I have the burden of hope
You have the luxury to walk out
I have the burden of a tightrope
You have the luxury to sit
I have the burden to stand
You have the luxury to quit
I have the burden to do what I can

(902)

Companions

You never helped me build
You always kicked over my blocks
You never shared a positive word
You only made me feel small
You spent every dime I earned
You showed me how I would fail
never how I could succeed
You said you loved me,
but your actions were of hate
You talk about fairy tales
but never how to truly succeed
You take all you can from me, money,
strength, confidence, hope
I thought you were my companion
But you were a hinderance

(903)

On Her Couch

Sitting on her couch we examined each other's eyes
I held her hand and complimented her smile, she blushed
She leaned towards me, we kissed, we dissolved
into our kiss
I pulled her closer to me she pushed me away
"Why, what's wrong?" I asked.
"Nothing, that was amazing. You're a good kisser."
She blushed.

I lightly tugged her arm she jumped into my embrace, and we surrendered to our kiss.

(904)

Delusion of Power

Evil shows a fake power it gives a false sense of strength
It uses fear to attempt to weaken the strong and destroy the fearful
True power, Godly power isn't loud or flamboyant. It is just present
Breaking through lies, and deceptions revealing love and hope.
Demonic power makes people think they're in control
While the Godly know they don't have any power God controls everything.

(905)

Unscripted

Life is unscripted, unplanned, uncensored
There isn't a right thing to say or do
There are just choices and actions
There is only love and pain
There is only hope and despair
There is, only strength and weakness
(906)

What's Real

Exhaustion is real
Frustration is real
Stress is real
Love is real
Peace is real
Taking a break is needed
Talking is useful
Being alone is peaceful
Journaling is helpful
Honesty with self and others
is important
Having a private life is serenity
Experimenting rounds out life
(907)

Repetition

I feel I'm repeating myself
Am I repeating myself because that's all I know
or is it what's important to me
Am I repeating myself because I'm that shallow
or because I'm afraid to go deeper
Am I repeating myself because
I don't want to be offensive
or because I want to be friendly
Am I repeating myself because I want to be seen
as a nice guy or because
I don't want to scare anyone away
am I repeating myself because I want to be seen
as a hero or because
I don't want to be seen as a villain

(908)

Young Love

Jake and Erin were in their forties when they first spoke
to each other at Starbucks getting their morning coffees. He had a
black coffee with only sugar, and Erin had a
macchiato.
They both chuckled when a new customer stumbled over
placing his order. Normally it would annoy them, but his
mispronunciation made them both laugh. They
caught each other's gaze and began to flirt.
Ten years later they were still playful and could
make each other laugh like teenagers.

(909)

Light Pollution

We used to only focus on the distant lights.
We used them to navigate our world and our lives
now we concentrate on the lights nearest to us.
Even when the close lights hurt and wound us
we still choose them over the more accurate ones.
To us, the little dem lights surrounding us are more
important than the distant bright lights.

(910)

Stop Stopping

I do want to change,
I do want a better life
But I want it easy,
I don't want to do the hard work
I want maturity,
I want wealth,
I want an easy life
But I don't want to do the heavy lifting
(911)

Next Level

Climbing the mountain, I slipped and slid near
the bottom. Climbing again but not from the bottom.
I finally reached the summit bruised and scarred
but wiser.
I think I can rest but there is another hill
ahead of me.
(912)

The Same

Rich and poor live the same lifestyle
Happiness and sadness are the same emotion
Good and bad are the same actions
High status and low status are the same character
A madman and a genius use the same words
The only thing that makes the difference is the heart
(913)

Somewhere

Somewhere our paths crossed
but we never saw one another
One day we looked into each other's eyes
but didn't say "Hi."
One time you asked for directions,
and I gladly helped
I walked my route alone searching for a love
Our streets merged but we didn't walk together
We conversed and laughed
and shared a short stroll on our path
We met again somewhere along the way,
we conveyed our feelings, and walked together

(914)

Cherries in Bloom

Fresh Cherries are ripe for picking
Sweet delicate flavor bursting with each bite
Juices drowning tastebuds with every nibble
Sticky sweetness glazing hungry lips
Delicious cherry aroma fills the air
Fresh young cherries ready to be harvested
and devoured

(915)

Master Plan

No plan will solve every problem,
but a plan can solve your problem.
The plan is a living entity.
It shifts, changes, moves.
Plans grow and mature
The lifeblood of a plan is action
Bugs and viruses will attack your plan
you must be diligent
For it to succeed

(916)

A Day

A day, a night
A stroll, a rest
A whisper, a kiss
A love, a feast
A family, a nest
A home
(917)

Response

The world doesn't respond to thoughts or ideas
The world responds to consistent action
The people who get noticed are the ones that
are working
The world only cares what you have to say
when action is your speech
More people are interested in receiving awards
than they are in doing the work to get the awards.
People want to be recognized as being the best
but they're too lazy to do the work
(918)

Playground

Kids burned off the stress of the day
on the playground
Alliances were made,
teams assembled,
battles won and lost
Screams of laughter,
cries of pain,
tests of courage
friendships forged

(919)

The Tongue

The tongue is sharp, sharper than you think
It can cut out a man's heart with a whisper
The tongue is harsh, harsher than a thought
It can wound a man's brain
The tongue is bitter, more bitter than life
It can scar the soul
The tongue is dangerous, more dangerous than a plan
It can shorten the user's lifespan

(920)

Fireworks

Your touch is fireworks on the Fourth of July
Explosions of joy,
beautiful colors flashing,
a celebration of our intimacy

(921)

One More Thing

I've been on my phone for too long. I'll put it down
Oh, wait I need to look up something.
An hour later, I'm tired of being on my phone,
let I'll put it down
Oh, wait one more thing
I'll put down my phone now.
Oh, what were the words to that song?
Oh man, my eyes are tired.
What was that actor's name?
Six hours later I have a headache
I need to get off this phone for a while
Oh, wait...

(922)

Travel Partner

Wherever you go in this life you will always be your
companion.
You will always second-guess yourself, doubt yourself,
and encourage yourself.
If you climb the highest peaks or stay in the depths
of the valley you will be there every step of the way.
If you're bored with yourself
everyone else will be bored with you
You can never get out of your head
So, make sure you have something interesting
to think about
(923)

Hello

Hello, can you hear me?
Yes, I hear you. Who're you trying to get hold of?
I'm looking for you.
Me? Why me, how can I help you?
I was told by a mutual friend
that you can handle a situation I have.
I don't know why you were sent to me.
I'm not in that line of work anymore.
Well, if you change your mind, you can contact me
at this number. I have to search for someone
who's able to complete this job.
Good luck.

(924)

Bills

Bills and debts
Fines and penalties
Owe and obligation
Solutions and answers
Plans and strategies
Ideas and options
(925)

Value Pact

Morale

Honesty

Hope

Confidence

Trust

Belief

Loyalty

Courage

Interdependence

Love

(926)

Drowsy

Midnight
Can't keep my eyes open
Yawning, every two seconds
I don't want to lie down
Sleeping, I will miss part of my life
I haven't had fun today
My mind wants to stray
(927)

Fat Ass

Everyone tries to shove food down my throat
Every time every meal
Have some more, eat more, have another plate
What is it about me that says I'm a fat ass
I eat as much as I want
One plate and I'm done
At first, everyone was telling me I ate too much.
to leave some food for other people,
I'm a human refrigerator
Now they are telling me to eat more,
that I'm not eating enough
What is it about me that says I'm a fat ass
Maybe they miss having someone that they can ridicule

(928)

Success is not a Destination

You develop success as you work toward your goal
You build success as you improve your skills
Success evolves over time
(929)

Showing Up

Be there for you.
Show up for you.
Be your own hero
Stand for yourself
Don't wait for anyone
No one is waiting for you
Be there for you.
Show up for you.
Be your own hero
Stand for yourself
(930)

The Road to Success

When I stepped onto the road chattering monkeys surrounded me, their constant noise breaking my concentration.
They were a constant source of irritation.
But I pressed on.
A mountain rose in front of me the height was intimidating but I climbed inch by inch. Finally reaching the summit I slipped off the edge of a cliff. Reaching behind me I grabbed the root of a tree and pulled myself up.
Carefully looking around I found a stable-ish bridge.
Despite doubt filling my mind I crossed the rickety bridge.
I arrived at a lake thinking this may be my end because I didn't know how to swim. While looking for sticks to build a fire I found a boat, but no oars. I tied three sticks together which I used to row across.
The farther I traveled the more obstacles I had to conquer. I noticed some are meant to distract me and some were meant to stop me. Besides the nagging monkeys there were sneaky snakes I quickly learned which one were pests and which ones were venomous.
There isn't an end to the road just another milestone.

(931)

We Argue

We argue, we fight, we bicker
We have to decide if we are going through normal
relationship issues or if this is something more toxic.
We need each other to win in life
But if we decide we are too toxic then
we have to manage alone

(932)

July 7 7:07

We met on July seventh at seven o seven a.m.
I was nervous about being a father
and you didn't know anything about
the world to have fears.
You looked at me with your soft brown eyes
my fears and hopes for you exploded in my mind.
I couldn't stop my hopes and dreams
of whom we'd become.
(933)

Love Broke Me

Love made me smile then it destroyed me
Love made me laugh then it made me cry
Love made me strong then it made me weak
Love made me friends then it left me lonely
Love made me hope then it filled me with despair
Love took me on a journey then it left me stranded
Love took me to the mountain top then kicked me off
Love made me courageous then it made me doubt
Love built me up then it broke me

(934)

Time Travel

Man won't be able to travel through time. Because the movement of the universe
The location of the universe is different than it was one hundred years ago, and in a week, it'll be in an another location.
Traveling through time not only affects the date but also the location of the Earth, the Sun, and the stars in the sky
To go forward in time will be to go where the Earth will be at a certain date so it might be possible
To travel backwards would be to go where the Earth used to be. While you're trying to go backwards in time you're also going forward because your actions are future actions, so you would be staying in the same time while everything around you move forward causing you be lost in space trapped time because if you stop trying to go backwards the Earth won't be there and you'll drift in space.

(935)

Who Am I to Me

I can't think about myself without thinking about others
What do I want them to think of me
What have others told me about me
What are the positive and negative things people have said about me
None of that matters. What matters is what I think about myself.
Who am I to myself
A son
A brother
A father
A poet
A writer
Those are still who I am to others.
Who am I to me

(936)

Becoming a father

A day, a night,
a weekend of delight
Hand holding,
eye gazing,
romantic playing
Smiles, laughter,
news of becoming a father
(937)

Lonely Man

Love became bickering, bickering became fighting, and fighting became lonely days
I went from having a four-course dinner to soup in a cup
Body heat became cold sheets
Coffee and conversation became java on the run
I love yous faded into the open air
Flowers and candy no longer have meaning
A connected couple became a lonely man
(938)

Just Write

Write through my doubt
Write through my fear
Write through my confusion
Write through my hopelessness
Write through my loneliness
Write through my blocks
Write through my unbelief
Write through my boredom
(939)

My Truth

I blame my dad for not being around
I blame my mom for being closed off
I blame myself for not growing beyond them
(940)

Pets

My first was a tabby
Next was a German Shepard
Then a goldfish
Parakeet
Lastly a puppy
Now my woman
is my pet
(941)

The Pale Blue Dot

Heroes and cowards
have all lived and died
on this ball of water and dirt
that is being pulled through space
by a sun that is in the event horizon
of a galaxy
which is being dragged
by the great attractor
(942)

What are Your Thoughts?

I know the thoughts I have of you,
your face, your voice, and your figure
where I'd like to take you,
What I'd like us to do
What are your thoughts about me?
Do I make you smile
What do you want us to do
Where do you want us to go
What are your private feelings of me
(943)

Busy Brain

My mind is too active, reading, writing,
and planning
It's becoming overwhelming
That is the purpose of the brain to move me
forward in my life
But overstimulation is causing me to burn out
I need quiet I need to put down my phone
and let my mind drift
Nothing to read, nothing to watch,
no music to listen to, no conversations
Just the wind, the water, and me

(944)

Home

When I hear the politicians,
I want to leave this city and state
When I walk along the lake
I want to live here forever
When I hear about the crime in my city
I want to run for my life
When I see the beautiful trees and smell the fresh air,
I want to soak up all their goodness
When I hear about the failing communities,
I want to find somewhere better
When I see all the amazing artwork,
I'm proud to stay where I am
Do I pay attention to my ears or my eyes

(945)

Carousel

A carousel circling the same spot
not advancing only the same up and down
the same round and round
Slow and steady all around
no growth no change just the same old circle

(946)

It Is Today

It is today
It is the time
It is the moment
Right now,
We forgot our future
We can't look forward to our past
All we have is this second
once it's gone,
we'll never have another chance
All we have is this second to love,
this second to help, this time to build.
We don't know our last second
We need to use the seconds we have
before they run out
(947)

Sailing

We set sail together
drifting among the stars
Sailing through space
on love and hope
we don't know if we'll make it
to a distant star
so, we keep drifting together
(948)

Too Shy

Too shy, too passive, too much of a people pleaser
to risk rocking society
Too shy, too passive, too much of a people pleaser
to change the world
Too shy, too passive, too much of a people pleaser
to fight for what's right
Too shy, too passive, too much of a people pleaser
to hurt feelings
Too shy, too passive, too much of a people pleaser
to run into danger
Too shy, too passive, too much of a people pleaser
to give true love

(949)

My Weapon

My weapon is my words
My sword and my shield
My weapon is my words
They defend and kill
My weapon is my words
They destroy and build
My weapon is my words
They bring order and chaos
My weapon is my words
They strengthen and weaken
My weapon is my words
They give hope and despair
My weapon is my words
They bring fear and faith
My weapon is my words
They heal and they hurt
My weapon is my words
They love and they hate
(950)

Disheveled

My organized mind is in disarray
Tumbled and turned searching for the right way
How much should I say, what should be unsaid
Should I revive the past or leave it dead
Should I stand still or should I be gone
Make repairs or leave things broken

(951)

Was it Love

Did we feel love or were we just horny
Did we feel love or were we just lonely
Did we feel love or were we just bored
Did we feel love or were we tired of being ignored
Did we feel love or did we just want a friend
Did we feel love or did we just want to blend in
Did we feel love or did we just want kids
Did we feel love or did we just want to release liquid
Did we feel love and have something to give
Did we feel love and were trying to be productive
Did we feel love and want to grow
Did we feel love or did we have something to show
Did we feel love

(952)

Serenity

She walked into the coffee shop. Soft brown skin, straight black hair, athletic figure, and an outfit revealing her weekly efforts in the gym.

She smiled at the barista, and she laughed at a personal joke between them.

Coffee in hand she turned and looked for a seat. She looked into my eyes. I pointed to the open chair in front of me. She smiled and approached.

"Thank you. It's so crowded in here today."

"Yes, it is. You're welcome. My name is Stone."

"Hi, Stone. I'm Serenity."

"Serenity? What a pretty name"

"You're cute, Stone."

"Thanks, I could use some Serenity in my life."

"Okay, Stone, that was corny."

We both laughed and talked till it was time for us to go to our jobs.

(953)

Move at Your Own Risk

Safety is elusive
Kindness is optional
Wealth is a scam
Friendship is conditional
Love is action
Trust is doubtful
Hope is work
(954)

To Me

To the me, I used to be, sorry I had to leave you behind
but for me to grow, I must let go of all the weak parts
To the me, I used to be, I must be more caring and less selfish
To the me, I used to be, for the man to grow the child must understand
To the me, I used to be, growth is scary but necessary
I must let go of the easy and familiar
To the me, I used to be, farewell

(955)

Calm in the Chaos

Chaos seems random and unstructured, but all these
random events are connected to one big outcome
Chaos can be the route that must be taken,
or it can be planned
Look for the calm in the chaos keep what connects
disregard the rest
Things that start in unison will eventually seem to
become chaotic but time will bring them back
Things that start chaotic will reveal their alignment
over time

(956)

I Remember

I remember your smile
I remember gazing into your eyes
I remember the smell of your perfume
I remember our hugs
I remember your voice
I remember our kisses
I remember your invitation
I remember your submission
I remember our passion
I remember our afterglow
I remember our promise
I remember our love
(957)

Humility

I was humbled by your beauty
I was humbled by your compassion
I was humbled by your philosophy
I was humbled by your honesty
I was humbled by your sincerity
(958)

Promises

Rage in her eyes, fire in her voice
You promised me companionship
You promised me safety
You promised me financial security
But your promises are starting to slip
I appreciate your hard work to improve our lives.
We no longer talk, or have our date nights,
you're always on the go.
I don't feel safe here anymore.
(959)

Nope

I saw a hottie walking my way
I said "Hi."
She said "Nope."
I said, "My name is Stone, what's yours?"
She said "Nope."
"Can I get your number?"
"Nope."
"Can I take you on a date?"
"Nope."
"Can I buy you a drink?"
"Nope."
When I sat in my Saab.
She asked, "Can I get a ride?"
I said, "Nope." And stepped on the gas.

(960)

New Normal

Changing your life doesn't mean making
one change once
it isn't magic where it just happens
It means changing your habits
Don't see changing your life as a final result
but as constant growth.
It isn't going to be easy
but it will be worth the effort
Don't look at exercising as something you
must do but as a way of life.
It's a part of your daily activities
it's a part of who you are.
It is your new normal no matter what anyone says
Or how anyone tris to belittle you
(961)

Repercussions

You think I'm not with your mother
because of the other woman. You need to understand
I had to leave before she destroyed me.
Our fights were mental and physical. I swore I'd never hit
a woman, but she never promised not to hit me.
I had to break our vow because she shattered our home
If I were single living alone in my own apartment, I still
wouldn't get back with her.

(962)

The River

On top of a hill, we enjoyed our meal alfresco.
I spoke of love's meaning and presented a ring
She told me no, she loves another
My heart exploded, tears billowed pain broke
the dam
I tried picking up the pieces of my heart,
but they were washed away before I could start
My pain became a river of hurt
depleting my love and my salt

(963)

The Conqueror

I was shy and afraid
You taught me how to stand
I was timid and had no voice
You helped me find my words
I was scared to stand my ground
You helped me find the courage to be a man
I was lost in life's issues
You guided me to the right path
I was always defeated in my mind
You counseled me to be a conqueror
I felt loveless and alone
You advised me to love myself
and find happiness in my company
You counseled me to be a conqueror
and how to defeat every doubt
You taught me how to live from the heart

(964)

Wild Horses

Running free, running wild, living on the edge,
full of courage and power
We were wild horses, living life on the edge
We took every risk we tried every challenge.
We let adventure rule our lives.
We were wild horses, living life on the edge
We faced every danger we were bold
and foolish, we tested life. We experimented
with love, we played with chances.
We were wild horses, running free,
running wild living on the edge,
full of courage and power
Our youth is gone our strength has faded
we share our memories of our freedom and foolishness
we were wild horses, running free,
running wild living on the edge,
full of courage and power

(965)

The Battle

Facing each other fighting to be the champion
Older more experienced and powerful
younger more energetic and with a longer reach
Punches landed, blood flowed
It ended in a draw
Title maintained
Rematch proclaimed

(966)

Measurements

Your height is determined by your actions
Your depth is determined by your studies
Your width is determined by your generosity

(967)

Pearls

It takes time for pearls to form
It takes experience to know which clams
are ready to be harvested
It takes effort to dig them out
It takes knowledge to know which pearls
have the highest value
It takes courage to share the pearls
with those who will see their worth.

(968)

I Accept Responsibility

I accept responsibility for my failures
I accept responsibility for the accidents I caused
I accept responsibility for disappointments
I accept responsibility for the heartbreak I've caused
I accept responsibility for being irresponsible

(969)

Push Through

Push through the darkness
Push through the self-doubt
Push through the naysayers
Push through the fears
Push through self-sabotage
Push through the tears
Push through giving up
Push through expectations
Push through long nights
Push through weakness
Push through and fight
(970)

Your Itinerary

Can you show me your
itinerary for your goals
Where did you start
Where are you going
What route are you taking
What is your ETA
(971)

I Want Distractions

I want to be distracted
but I'm bored with distractions
Do I need a focus point
Do I need quiet
My mind is so cluttered
How can I declutter my mind
I have so many worries and fears
How can I unstress my mind
I need a distraction

(972)

The Path of Most Resistance

Don't be like water
don't follow the path of least resistance
Be like a bodybuilder lift the heaviest weight possible
Don't look for the easy route
look for the hard path
The easy way fools you into thinking life gives you anything you want
But struggle shows you that to get what you want takes effort

(973)

Everything is Okay

Stress can break you mentally and physically.
Stress is caused by not seeing a solution to your situation
Sometimes the answer is to be honest
even if it's scary or will cause pain
Sometimes the answer takes more searching
Sometimes the is to do nothing
Everything will be okay if you are confident and bold
Sometimes the solution is to stick with your plan no
matter how boring or how long it's seeming to take.

(974)

Accepting My Negative Mind

Everyone says to fight your negative mind,
but I believe we need to accept it
it is part of us deep down,
it rises to the top when we face new obstacles

We mustn't follow its words or actions. It can be our excuse to fail, to give up, or not even try.

These statements can't be truly defeated because they
are part of us, and to fight against them is fighting
against ourselves

Our positivite mind is also a part of us we must accept and call on it for the courage to grow

The best thing we can give the world is our-authentic-selves

I accept that the negative thoughts will arise I will see what is the reason for the negativity is it something legitimate or just an excuse then I'll take the right action.

(975)

Anger Issues

Your rage is another's amusement
Your hate makes others laugh
When people know your buttons,
they will push them so they can laugh at you
Others will use your triggers
to make you shoot yourself
While you're furious over the smallest thing
they will get advances
Your lack of self-control allows other to puppet you
(976)

It’s Only Money

So many people are worried about money
But it’s just like water. It goes out it comes back
We are in control of where the money goes
and what happens to it when it returns
Our fears control how we react but if we accept
the fact that it's only money like electricity
for it to be affective it must complete a circuit
it must go out complete a task and return

(977)

Playmate

We met in the playground and quickly became friends
We ran, we laughed, we played tag
We climbed the monkey bars then jumped down,
and we slid down the slide
We quickly became friends and never exchanged names
We ran, we laughed, and we played till the sky became
dark
We had our adventures in the park.

(978)

Alone or Lonely

She said she was lonely
she wanted someone to love
She wanted a companion
someone to share her world
Coworkers were fine
but she wanted someone in her home
In the beginning, being alone was fun
but soon loneliness crept into her heart
Being alone was good for following her dreams
but loneliness made her question red flags
Being alone she achieved a lot,
being lonely she broke her own heart.
She said she was lonely
she wanted someone to love
She wanted a companion
someone to share her world
(979)

Good Morning

May your morning start with
Thirty minutes of quiet
Energy to pursue your goals
And a cup of coffee in your hand
(980)

It's Gonna Suck

Working through hard times
Turning away from family
and friends and connections
Ignoring naysayers
Enduring the haters
Surviving the loneliness
For someone who didn't study
in school to have to study
to be successful, it's gonna suck
But the effort will pay off
(981)

Self-motivation

Self-motivation is hard to maintain
Especially when negativity lives in your house
Self-motivation is hard to find
When you don't know where to search
Self-motivation is a necessity for success
You must make the foundation deep and wide
Self-motivation is part of your daily grind
(982)

Justifications

We have a desire to be accepted
and to receive that acceptance
we will try to explain our reasoning
or thought process
We may even feel bad
if people say they don't understand us
causing us to try to explain more
causing us stress, worry, and fear
when we realize that we don’t have to justify
our actions or thoughts
we just need to work on our ideas

(983)

Wishful Thinking

Dreams, fantasies, desires
Freebies, handouts, free rides
Wanting, expectancy, yearning
Wishes, longings, eagerness
(984)

Destination

The journey builds.
Discipline
Confidence
Compassion
Bravery
Tough skin
The destination brings.
Victory
Celebration
And sadness
(985)

Beans and Rice

Brian was chastised for cursing when he was younger

he started saying, “I don't give a hill of beans.”

his friends playfully teasing him called him “Beans.”

Rachel an albino was often bullied and called “white rice,” by the bullies in her neighborhood.

She some of her bullies ended up at the same college with her. To take the sting from the bullies Rachel

shortened it to Rice.

Brian and Rachel met in history class began dating and became known as Beans and Rice. Brian joined the football team; Rachel joined the track team.

(986)

Heatwave

One hundred seven degrees in the shade
humidity siphoning all the moisture from my body
Sun rays are baking my skin like
I'm the main course on the menu
The air conditioner is working triple time to make
my room feel like a freezer.
In the winter I begged for summer
now I'm begging for cooler temperatures
I don't want Subzero temps
just slightly cooler than one hundred

(987)

Jerkitude

My arrogance makes me think
I'm better than others
Illiteracy makes me think I'm smarter
Laziness makes me think I'm more skilled
Lust has me believing all women want me
(988)

The Desperado

Out of desperation
He withdrew his six shooter
Demanded the banks cash
He jumped on his Harley
And fled the city
(989)

The Firefighter

Rita was flashy, Versace, Hermes, and Baccarat Rouge.
She was single, no man wanted the maintenance
She lived with her parents, her goal to move to downtown Chicago.
An accidental fire trapped her in her room
She screamed and panicked, she thought she was doomed
Jake, a fireman, broke in and carried her to safety
Her high-end clothes, gone. Her fragrances boiled away
She didn't care because she was alive

Her favorite scent is now smoke and ash. She was afraid she was gonna die but in an instant, she was carried to safety by a man she now loves.

He was single too, and not looking, women and some men proposed to him.

Rita was an excellent cook from her mom. She
volunteered at the firehouse to cook their meals.
The firefighters teased her, but her heart
belonged to Jake.

(990)

Stop Staring at Me

Stop staring at me
Stop watching me
I'm just being me
Stop staring at me
Com-on Walk with me
Sit and talk to me
But don't stare at me
I'm just being me
I have grown a bit
But deep down I'm still me
Stop staring at me
I may have grown a bit
But deep down I'm still me
(991)

Ego

What is my depth
What is my height
What makes me better
What makes me right
What is my depth
What is my height
What makes my day bright
What makes it night
What is my depth
What is my height
(992)

Moving Fast

moving fast and moving strong
moving to get the work done
moving fast and moving strong
Moving to build a life in the sun
moving night and moving day
moving in time from place to place
Moving in life at life's pace
(993)

Self-Praise

Self-praise is not arrogance
Praising yourself because you
have or are reaching a goal
that you set for yourself is not
against anyone
Arrogance is thinking and
acting like you're better than
other people.
If other people's feelings get
hurt because you speak of
your achievements then they
are disappointed with
themselves.
(994)

Summer

For Father's Day,
my daughter gave me
a German Shepherd puppy
I named her Summer.
I had another daughter to raise.
Her energy kept me moving
I didn't have time to be lazy
Was I training her or was she my trainer

(995)

Good Luck Charm

Going to work the morning of my birthday, I found a
penny head side up with my birth year stamped on the
top
I stuck it in my pocket and went on my way
I ran into my high school crush we hugged and chatted. She remembered it was my birthday and kissed me on
the lips then she had to go to work.
Grinning from ear to ear I continued my walk I met my
best friend who told me happy birthday and handed me
a hundred-dollar bill.
He had to run some errands and headed off to make his
runs.
When I arrived at my job I was told to go to the
lunchroom. There was a cake with candles on the table
most of my coworkers were there and sang happy
birthday.
Then someone honked their horn. I was standing in the
middle of the street looking at the penny and I had to run
to work so I wouldn't be late.

(996)

You Were the One

You were the only one I wanted, all I ever needed
You were the one who made me smile when it was
needed
You were the one who made my days brighter
You were the one who made me want to be greater
You were the one who taught me how to love
You were the one who fit me like a glove
You were the one I wanted to marry
You were the one who waited even though I tarried
(997)

Stress

I don't earn enough to cover these bills
Creditors are calling demanding more than
I can afford
School fees on the rise
Wife complaining kids crying
Where do I find relief
Debts high, pay low
It's enough stress to make you want to go.
How do you earn more, how do you juggle
complaining kids, and a crying wife
The wife wants your time but, cries cause there's
no money to enjoy life
Millionaires spent more time, in the beginning
working than with their families.
Family time came later and fuller

(998)

A White Beard and Wrinkles

A white beard from worry
Wrinkles from confusion
A white beard from doubt
Wrinkles from hopelessness
A white beard from no stress relief
Wrinkles from frowning
A white beard from looking for answers
Wrinkles from studying all night
A white beard and wrinkles for love
(999)

Feel So Good

When I started this challenge,
I would get a hit of dopamine with each poem I wrote
The more poems I wrote the less dopamine I'd receive because writing every day was becoming a habit.
As I started formatting the first volume, I'd get another hit of dopamine each day. By the time I started formatting the second volume
the dopamine became less
but it was too much of a habit to stop.
Dopamine rewards you for your achievement, until it
becomes a habit and you don't need it to keep going.

(1,000)

The Other Woman

She asked for my number
I said I had a wife
She said she didn't mind
she just wanted to be a part of my life
I said I'm faithful
She feigned disappointment
I shrugged and walked away

(1,001)

A Date

A smile, a hug, a kiss
A pen and paper, a list
A plan, a schedule, a date
Anxious, nervous, the wait
Family, the flowers, the aisle
The dress, the train, the veil
Music, standing, the stride
The roses, the ring,
the bride coming,
accepting,
The priest,
the eyes,
the vow
(1,002)

Romantic

Sitting in my home office at my computer
Formatting my next book
I didn't notice when she came in
She kissed me on my cheek
I turned in surprise
She kissed my lips and smiled
She pushed my chest my office chair rolled back
She sat on my lap,
wrapped her arms around my neck
I wrapped my arms around her waist,
we kissed
She melted into my arms
I carried her into the bedroom

(1,003)

Suga Daddy

I wanted a companion
She wanted extra money
We discussed our boundaries
No hanky-panky, no touchy-feely
I wanted a woman
I could share some days with
But not the nights. She teased.
We joked and grew closer
We had breakfasts, lunches,
and adventures
She surprised me one day
with a peck on the lips
The kiss soon became our routine
a peck before we part
One long adventurous day
she asked if she could spend the night
I agreed and that night we didn't sleep
Our relationship had changed
she moved in with me

(1,004)

Artwork

She is a work of art
Her beauty begins in her heart
and shines through her eyes
Her compassion shows in her face
Her confidence is heard in her voice
She is a work of art
Her neck long and elegant
Her shoulders delicate
Her chest voluptuous
Her waist soft concave curves
Her hips gently spreading
Her thighs thick and smooth
Her calves curvy and strong
Her feet graceful and feminine

(1,005)

Champagne and Chicken Salad

To celebrate our upcoming victory,
I bought champagne and chilled it in the fridge
Next to some chicken salad from the night before
The victory we achieved we invited friends to celebrate
The time came and went
We were disheartened when no one showed
I was going to dump the champagne,
but she said I shouldn't waste my money
We were still hungry after eating the hors d'oeuvres
She took out the chicken salad and crackers and we washed it down with the champagne.
We watched a movie and slept on the couch.

(1,006)

Up and At'em

Get up before the alarm
Get up and plan the day
Get up and move fast
Get up and do the work
Get up and get it done
Get up and get at'em
(1,007)

I'm Starving

I'm starving, my stomach is rumbling
I need a meal, nothing sweet
I'm hungry, I have a goal that must be fed
I'm starving for success
My stomach is rumbling for knowledge
I need a meal of experience
I'm hungry to reach my goal
I'm starving for success
(1,008)

Enthusiasm

A lack of enthusiasm may affect the quality of your work
I'm not talking about, your, lack of enthusiasm
but rather the enthusiasm of those who supported you
Their lack of interest it may demotivate you.
You have to remember it is your dream
You must stay encouraged to see it through
Don't show others your progress even if they ask.
Just tell them you're still working on it.
Let them find out with the rest of the world.

(1,009)

Word Smith

I use my pen to shape and mold my words
like a blacksmith uses his hammer on steel
I use my eraser and white out to carve intricate details
on my paper like a sculptor uses a chisel and hammer
to chip away stone
I use my pen to design landscapes with my words
like an artist using a paintbrush on a canvas
I am a smith, a sculptor, an artist of words.

(1,010)

The Fox

Slick and wiry
Fast and cunning
opportunistic
Sees a solution
in any situation

(1,011)

Memories

She showed me pictures of our life together.
Before we married, before our daughter,
before we both gained weight.
I smiled at the memories, but I didn't re-feel the feeling.
There was too much hurt, too many lies, too much
manipulation to rekindle the love I once had for her.
The memories were fun to see but the re-love would
never be.

(1,012)

I Called You Brother

We fought on the playground side-by-side
We fought on the block back-to-back
We even stood against each other toe-to-toe
But I'll always call you brother
even when we don't see eye-to-eye
We stood together in war
We were each other's best man
when we found the women, we loved
I called you, acquaintance, I called you,
friend, I called you... brother
(1,013)

I Remember Why

I remember why I fell in love
Your smile, your compassion,
your understanding
I remember why I fell in love
Your hugs, your kisses, your surrender
I remember why I fell in love
Your touch, gentle, comforting, tender
I remember why I fell in love
My safe place, my sounding board,
my defender
I remember why I fell in love
The breakfasts, lunches, and dinners
I remember why I fell in love
Walks in the park, carnival rides,
and adventures
I remember why I fell in love

(1,014)

Lack of Loyalty

She invited her ex to her birthday party
and he showed up.
She didn't understand why her current boyfriend
was mad and took back his gift and left.
The woman was bold enough to invite her ex
and the ex was comfortable enough to show up.
Neither one of them had respect for the current boyfriend.
So, he respected himself.
He didn't simp and "okay," the situation.
He did right!

(1,015)

Kiss The Wind

I blow kisses to the wind
Hoping they find you
I blow kisses to the wind
Because I miss you
I blow kisses to the wind
You were my heart
I blow kisses to the wind
Wishing we could restart
I blow kisses to the wind
In search of you
(1,016)

Blue Sky

The blue of the sky seems so far away
The elevation of a plane brings it into reach
Just outside your window inches from your hand
The clouds are so high above the Earth
You can't touch what's inside until they burst
In an open-top plane, you can feel the wet before it rains
The blue sky where the birds fly
free from the congestion of the city
Fresh air no worries just open and free.

(1,017)

Dead End

You've hit the wall
You can't advance any more
You try to climb
But you hit your head
The ceiling is low
you'll need someone to raise the ceiling
you need a friend, an ally
someone that has climbed through the ceiling
(1,018)

Confusion

I don't know what to write. I don't know what to say.
words come to my mind, but then they fly away
Should I say this, or should I say that?
Should I say something powerful or not?
So many words so many thoughts so many feelings
So many directions to go all of these ideas are appealing
(1,019)

Flirting

She mentions her boyfriend every time we meet
She talks about how much she likes him
and how he's so sweet
And then she flirts with me
I can't tell if she's being friendly or does,
she wants to be with me.
She talks like she's interested
like she wants to be more than just friends
But then she brings up her boyfriend again
I'll stay in the friend zone and let her have her man
I'm too old for playing games. I'll just stand where I am.

(1,020)

My Cravings

I crave silence for hours maybe a day
I crave solitude to write, to think,
to let my mind wander.
I crave alone time no conversations,
no questions, no communication
I crave to be unplugged no movies,
no TV, no phone
I crave quiet no music, no singing,
no sounds
Not forever just a few hours
so, my mind can reset

(1,021)

Stunted Growth

We've stunted our growth and shortened
our lifespan
The air used to be oxygen-rich and pure
Fumes and gases polluted the air causing us
to shrink and struggle to breathe
For us to live we have become parasites destroying
the thing that's keeping us alive

(1,022)

I Broke My Heart

I thought you were cute and sweet
You became the muse for my fantasies
We joked and had a few laughs
At night I stare at your photograph
I imagine a roll in the sheets
Only to discover you don't feel that way about me
I created a whole relationship in my mind
Now I have to stay away from you for a time
Allowing my heart to disconnect from you
preparing to connect with someone true

(1,023)

Pillows

Twelve straight hours, mind and body drained
Dinner is waiting I'm too tired to eat
Strip to my underwear and lie across the bed
My woman slips in next to me
and directs me to lie my head on her double Ds
Warm, soft, relaxing I doze off to sleep
I wake up eight hours later refreshed
and ready for the new day
"Thank you, baby. I needed the pillows last night."
"I know baby, you were so stressed and I knew they
would help."
Her double D pillows are the best.

(1,024)

New Life

Her egg settled in her womb
and waited to be fertilized
We shared a passionate night
I filled her with my love
My semen raced to her patient egg
One sperm cell entered
and mingled my DNA with hers
The cells divided and multiplied
A tiny human began taking shape
nine months of multiplying and growing
A new human entered the world
With new ideas and skills
to add to the world.

(1,025)

Next

The ladder of hope and love
Stretches to the clouds
You have to climb each rung
no matter the depth of your fear
Each rung is a new test, a new decision,
a new direction
Each level builds strength and character
The higher you climb the clearer your view
of what is important
There isn't a peak just another tier
Don't try to rush, it isn't about speed
It's about truth and honesty

(1,026)

Breaking the Old

Habits are what we consistently do
Bad habits are easier to fall into
seeking others' approval, we develop bad habits
And before we know it,
we're in a hole we can't get out of
Prioritize your success despite
what others may say
The work is hard, and your goal may seem
far away
Rewarding yourself for every achievement
Will rewrite your mindset

(1,027)

Reigniting Talent

Talent is like an eternal flame
It dims after long periods of non-use,
but it never goes out
To make the fire roar again
requires the fuel of action
A constant daily action
and skill improvement.

(1,028)

Written in Stone

Our names are chiseled in stone
forever combined
And like our love they're eternal
People will see our names and wonder
How long did our love last
We will know that it was forever
(1,029)

Chicago Summers

Chicago winters can get below zero degrees
Chicago summers can get over one hundred degrees
During Chicago winters, you look like a polar bear
During Chicago summers, you look like a nudist
During Chicago winters, you don't want to sweat
During Chicago summers, sweat is your ally
During Chicago winters, you can get a windburn
During Chicago summers, you can get a sunburn
During Chicago winters, you want to stay inside
During Chicago summers, you want to sleep under the stars

(1,030)

Crest

The journey to each summit has its challenges
getting you to the next peak asks the same question,
"Are you gonna stop here or continue your streak?"
Reaching the next zenith requires more study,
more practice, new skills
"Are you going to stop or continue up this hill?"
Stopping is a choice there isn't an ultimate top
There is only the next crest

(1,031)

Dinosaurs

They lived their lives
They roamed free
They dominated the world
When God decided the time was right,
he cleared the planet for us
Now all we know about these creatures
is what we learn from digging up their bones
We've had our time to live our lives
To roam free
and to dominate the world
God lets us decide when we're done
and we bury our old selves to be born again in him
We must leave our old ways buried in the dirt
and don't let anyone dig up our past
because we've accepted our past deeds and found our peace

(1,032)

Goodbye

She waved at me.
I waved back.
She blew me a kiss,
I laughed and caught it.
She boarded her plane
I whispered goodbye.
(1,033)

Closure

Sometimes closure isn't always possible.
Sometimes you have to accept the situation,
set boundaries, and move on
Closure isn't about looking to forgive,
that decision has already been made
You want to know, "why,"
You want closure so you can decide of extent
of your boundaries
sometimes boundaries must be set without closure
(1,034)

A Flask of Tequila

When my days seem like I've been in an arena
The only thing that helps is a flask of tequila
When I want a drink to go with my fajita
The only thing that works is a flask of tequila
When people berate my character
The only thing that calms me is a flask of tequila
When my tongue is dry like sandpaper
The only thing that helps is a flask of tequila
When I don't feel popular
The only thing that eases me is a flask of tequila

(1,035)

A Glimpse

A glimpse in your eyes and I'm mesmerized
A glimpse at your lips and my heart skips
A glimpse of your figure and my desire is triggered
A glimpse at your hips and my wood gets stiff
A glimpse of your face and I want to stay near you
(1,036)

The Center of My Universe

You called me Dada,
it shot straight to my heart
the name started with a bang
and spread in every direction
It filled the void that was my life
It sparked and flared sending
new life from my center
Filling my universe with love
(1,037)

I Never Knew

She had a crush on me
But I never knew
She waited years for me
But I never knew
She followed my life
But I never knew
She turned down men for me
But I never knew
She wrote songs for me
But I never knew
She came to my wedding
But I never knew
She cried day and night for me
But I never knew

(1,038)

A Day Off

No customer demands
Just a quiet walk in the park
No explaining company policy
Just jazz in the background
No problem solving
Just watching flitting birds
No Karen debates
Just a relaxing breeze
No manager meetings
Just a restful day off
(1,039)

Walking

A walk in the park
A walk on the beach
A walk on the city streets
A walk upstairs
A walk up a hill
A walk through the Catskills
A walk at night
A walk during the day
A walk with my bae
A walk to clear my mind
(1,040)

Some Cute Things

Puppies running
Kittens playing
Babies, trying to talk
A lion cub roaring
Panda cubs climbing trees
Babies laughing
Your smile
You blushing
The way you say my name
(1,041)

Impressions

People are not worth impressing
Only a few are worth your friendship
None are worth knowing your secrets
People don't laugh at your jokes they laugh at you
People are not worth impressing
Some only want to know your secrets
Some want to make you fail

(1,042)

A Friendship Smile

A friendly smile that says
"I'm glad to see you."
is so heartwarming
Knowing that your presence
brighten someone's day
improves your day
A smile not based on lust
or want, but simply because
you're you
A friendship smile makes life
worth living
Be the reason, someone smiles

(1,043)

Inglenook

Wrapped in a blanket
in the corner near the fireplace
is the perfect place to hide from
the subzero temperatures
Wrapped in your arms under
the covers chase the chill
from bones
Soft neck kisses give me chills
and raise my heat higher
The fireplace's warmth is nice
but cuddling sets my desire
on fire

(1,044)

Realness

Makeup hides the truth.
Makeup covers shame
Makeup is a disguise
Unless you make up your mind
Until you make up your heart
Revealing your unfiltered side.
(1,045)

Sweet to Sour

You were the sweetest girl I knew
Friendly, helpful, and kind
A gentleness and playfulness that made me laugh
As others started to pursue you
You weren't as kind
You became absorbed in guys chasing you
And lost who you used to be
I want you to be happy to find a man
you love but you seem more interested in what
you can get than who you can love

(1,046)

The Strength of the Warrior

The strength of the warrior
is not in his muscles, but in his heart
does he have the heart to continue the fight
when his physical strength is gone?
Does he have the heart to continue the fight
when his body is wrecked with pain?
does he have the heart to continue the fight
even though he's the last one standing?
Does he have the heart to continue to fight
till the end?

(1,047)

Early Sunset

Late sunrise, early sunset
Warm summer days fade
Cooler temperatures begin
Cuddle season starts
(1,048)

Free Days

Free days are
doing what you want
Working how you want
building what you want
Learning what you want
Living how you want
Loving how you want
Free days can be hard
But you can live the life you want
Free days are
peaceful days
(1, 049)

Construction

Shaping, forming, building
A new life
A new you
A new form
Once the old you is recognized
The new you has to be grown
New lessons
New studies
New development
New construction

(1,050)

A Billion Years

A billion years I've sailed through this darkness
A billion years whirling around this black hole
I feel the pull around this event horizon trying
to draw me in
While I've been a billion years on the edge
Some hitchhikers have surrounded me
Some are bigger than others with their hitchhikers
I was just a sun then I became a solar system
One of my hitchhikers has life, I hope they know
I'm flying to the center of this galaxy
one day I'll be there, and I can't escape
(1,051)

For Me

I've written for others short and long
I've written of hopes and dreams
I've written rhymes
I've written about fears and doubts.
I've spent enough time writing for others.
It's time for me to write about me
to write for myself and what I think

(1,052)

Feelings

So many choices, so many things to feel
So many directions, what path is right for me
What do I think? How should I feel?
What is my truth?
It is my real. It's what I feel.
all I can do is share my truth whether it's old or new
I learn as I grow and then I still don't know
(1,053)

God's Blessing

I don't want to say the wrong thing
for the sake of creativity
But I want to reveal God's goodness
in a unique way
I have been blessed to live sixty years
my brother didn't
I've been blessed to see my daughter grow up
My father wasn't around to see me become a man
hardships made me stronger and bolder
doubts have taught me to believe
fears have taught me courage
hate has taught me love
pain has taught me joy
uncertainty has taught me hope

(1,054)

Dusty Trail

I walked along the dusty trail
sad and alone
I walked along the dusty trail
with no place to call home
I walked along the dusty trail
every day of the week
I walked along the dusty trail
my confidence getting weak
I walked along the dusty trail
the rain slowly fell
I walked along the dusty trail
hardship broke me out of my shell
I walked along the muddy trail
Each day I grew
I walked along the dusty trail
Becoming new

(1,055)

The Antidote

The treatment for a cold is hot soup
The cure for a virus is no food and rest
The drug for sadness is a hug
The remedy for hate is compassion
The therapy for failure is iteration
The medicine for doubt is perseverance
The antidote for anxiety is understanding
The prescription for loneliness is companionship

(1, 056)

A Million Poets

A million poets, sharing their thoughts,
sharing their hearts, and their minds
A million poets, sharing their experiences,
dreams, and goals
A million poets, trying to change the world
with their stories
A million poets, saying the same thing
in a million different ways
A million poets sharing their thoughts,
their hearts, and their minds.

(1,057)

Shit... My Phone Died

Shit... My phone died in the middle of an argument
I was having with my wife.
Because the call ended so abruptly,
she may think she was right.
I heatedly expressed my thoughts,
but the call dropped before I made my point
She won't be picking me up tonight.
Shit, I gotta long walk.
Shit... My phone died in the middle of an argument
I was having with my wife.
Shit... I can't even call an Uber.
It's gonna be a long walk tonight.
You can't let a woman know when she's right.
She'll never let you live it down.
Shit... my phone died. I can't even apologize.

(1,058)

Custom Complaint

We often think others' complaining is worse than ours
But our complaints are more valid
Our complaints are specific to our situation
and emotions at that moment
We get frustrated with hearing the complaints
of others'
But we could complain for hours
If we have an audience or a sympathizer
We will ramble
Complaining or venting
Venting you express your frustration then work
To find the answer and improve
Complaining you say the same thing to as many people
as you can for sympathy

(1,059)

Mastery

Strength is not the absence of
Weakness but lifting despite it
Success isn't the absence of failure
but finding ways around it
Peace isn't the absence of
hardships but accepting them
Bravery isn't the absence of fear
it is acting in spite of it
Happiness isn't the absence of sadness
it's realizing they coexist
Love isn't the absence of anger
but understanding that anger is caused by misunderstandings
and love is finding answers

(1,060)

Just Write it Out

Late at night, mind won't turn off,
tossing and turning in the dark
Grab my journal and a pen I don't think about the words
Or the subject. I just write it out
I don't judge my words I just communicate them
to the paper.
My mind has something it wants to communicate.
I don't hold it in.
I write it out; I don't try to figure it out.
Whether it's a worry, doubt, poem, or story
just write it out

(1,061)

Doubts

Doubts and fears grow as I get closer to my goal
am I running out of what to say or am I just afraid?
Is lack of inspiration, stopping my writing,
or fear of succeeding?
My goal is over a week away,
and I don't know what to say.
Is it writer's block or fear?
Doubts flood my mind like in the days
when I first started this quest.
Do I have the words or talent to continue?

(1,062)

White Noise

The airport is the perfect place to zone out.
So much noise, so many voices
I don't have to focus on any one
My mind can wander and take its own journey
An unexpected word, half a sentence,
a laugh drifts in and out of my ears
It's all white noise and random sounds
I lose myself

(1,063)

Boredom

Boredom can be thinking the same thoughts over
and over
New thoughts fuel creativity.
Rehashing old thoughts, old memories, and old hurts
causes frustration and depression.
Traveling doesn't mean a long journey.
Going to a different neighborhood, a different beach,
or a new park can ignite new ideas
An idle mind is filled with hurt and lies.
Boredom can fill you with negativity or spark creativity
(1,064)

Panther

Sleek and black
Ready to pounce
Amber eyes glowing
scanning the prey
Looking for an easy target
The predator, waiting for its meal
(1,065)

Along the Lake

Riding my bike along the lake
I sit on a bench, taking a break
Walkers, runners, skaters, and cyclists
Some amateurs, some professionals
zipping on the same circuit
Some for health others to impress
Some for speed others just doing their best
Light blue sky, dark blue water
Nice scenery for a people watcher
Sailboats and speedboats in the distance
Wanting to take that chance
Breathing the fresh air, feeling the cool breeze
I stand and mount my bike it's time for me to leave

(1,066)

Happy for You

We walked hand in hand
We shared our life plans
Our conversations about a bright future
Became arguments of our past failures
We couldn't be together anymore
That's when I walked out the door
After years of deciding what to do
I realized the best part of my life was with you
I called to check on your life
And learned that you're a wife
My heart is broken in two
But I'm happy for you
I'm happy that you found a good love
I wish you all happiness from above

(1,067)

Is Pain the Answer

Is pain the answer to perfection
Is misery the solution to mastery
Is trauma the key to talent
Does agony bring out the awesome work
Does hurt, develop know-how

(1,068)

Boomerang

Words are like a boomerang they will return to you
Vibration shoots out from you and bounces back
Energy flows out and ricochets back
What you send into the world comes back to you
Whether negative or positive, ingratitude,
or gratitude it will rebound
Most times it'll comes back stronger than when it left
Don't send out what you don't want to come back to you

(1,069)

Contrast

On my way to celebrate a couple's seventy-fourth wedding anniversary,

I learned a cousin had died of a heart attack.

The contrast of life.

The husband is ninety-two she is eighty-nine

My cousin was forty-three years old

The contrast of life one life is extended, another is ended

The couple celebrated in the church, but my cousin died on the street while cleaning his car.

The contrast of life.

How can I feel happy for a couple's long life together

when my own cousin's life was cut short

(1, 070)

It's Personal

Life is personal
Love is personal
Kindness is personal
Success is personal
Failure is personal
Time is personal
Goals are personal
(1,071)

The Failure's Migraine

The failure's migraine is impatience
The failure's migraine is wanting instant gratification
The failure's migraine is wanting a lottery win
The failure's migraine is having something to prove
The failure's migraine is not making decisions
The failure's migraine is dreaming.

(1,072)

Execution

Take action
Do the work
Execute
Apply yourself
Action overcomes doubt
Working pushes away fear
Execution drowns loneliness
Application conquers naysayers
(1,073)

Top's Game

Top didn't like sports. Money was her game. It started
when she was ten and her brother was thirteen with
the Monopoly board game...
She lost every time they played. Her granddad once told
her. You have to learn the rules of the game. Everyone
wants to make money quickly but
the winner is who has the most money at the end.
Spending the last of your money to buy houses
and hotels can seem risky, but if you do it early you will collect rent the whole game.

She applied that idea to her real finances.

She started saving her birthday money, her allowance, and any money she earned by doing odd jobs for the
neighbors. It was weird to her how family made
suggestions for her money. You can buy a lot of candy with that, a lot of toys, or a pretty dress.

She didn't want any of that, she always thought about playing Monopoly
and what her granddad said, she wanted to buy an apartment building and rent it out. She tried telling Mary, her bestfriend, but she thought Top was daydreaming.

Mary wanted to spend the money on something flashy
and pretty.

Top's parents thought she was saving for college. She realized she would need to learn more about the rules
of money and she decided to take business courses.

She would read and learn everything she could about finance and real estate.

She tried to buy a two-flat when she turned sixteen but
no one would help her everyone saw her as a child
trying to be grown up too fast.

She decided she would buy her first building in two more
years.
Ten years later at twenty-eight she sold the two-flat and
purchased a rundown twenty-room motel. She took out
a business loan and had the property renovated.
Seven years later she purchased and renovated two
more motels. Her first plan was to sell these properties
and buy a large hotel but the motels were doing so well she expanded. Just like her grandad told her, buy a few
properties early and people will pay you during the
whole game, wealth isn't about how fast you make
money the winner is the one with the most money
at the end of the game.

(1,074)

Before

Before you become successful
you must believe you're successful
Before you believe you're successful
you must speak success
Before you speak of success
you must think of being successful
Before you think of being successful
God will show you the success you can have.
Before God can tell you of your successes
you must have an ear to hear
Before you have an ear to hear
you must be ready for a change in your life.

(1,075)

Money Tree

Money doesn't grow on trees,
but money does grow like a tree
You can't pluck money off a tree,
But you can live off the fruit of your investments
You can't plant money in the ground
and expect it to grow,
but it will grow in a stock,
or it can be seed for a business
Money, like trees takes time and care to grow

(1,076)

Killing Yourself

Don't kill yourself for a company
They will watch you die
Punch you out
Step over you
And assign someone else
to do the job you had
And give the promotion you were working
so hard for to someone less enthusiastic

(1,077)

Don't be so Black

Don't be so black that you don't
explore the world
Don't be so black that you live
in the same neighborhood all your life
Don't be so black that you blame other races
for your failures
Don't be so black that you think that you
have to succeed alone

(1,078)

Not Just Family

Not just family but also a friend
Someone who takes an interest
in your life and gives a hand
Not just family but also an inspiration
Someone who can help you through
your isolation
Not just family but also a helper
Someone who is in your corner
Not just family but someone closer
(1,079)

No Cares

No one cares about your tears
No one is worried about your issues
No one is concerned about your goals
No one thinks about your victories
or failures
Everyone will be mad at you for standing
on your boundaries
Everyone will take advantage
of your kindness
Everyone's thoughts
are on their own lives and problems
Build your empire for yourself
Get in shape for yourself
Work on yourself for yourself

(1,080)

Signs of Love

Sharing experiences
personal details
Encouragement
commitment
loyalty
Love language
quirks, and habits
Holding hands
Gifts for no reason
Comforting
(1,081)

Chirp, Chirp

Sitting on the porch eating a sandwich,
watching the sun slip below the horizon.
Thinking about my life; my job, my home,
my love, and what else is to come.
A soft chirp interrupts my thoughts.
I search for the tiny creature making the big sound.
It's probably in the fresh-cut grass calling to its mate.
The sky changes to hypnotic colors drawing my mind
to deepening feelings.
A chirp louder and this time seems closer
I scan again for this minuscule musician.
A brown finch hopping near my feet
I toss him a piece of bread,
he grabs it and flitters away

(1,082)

The First Day

I allowed myself to feel it was love instead
of what it was... lust.
I allowed myself to believe that she was feeling
the same for me.
I allowed myself to assume that her smiles
were affection
I allowed myself to think she wanted me
like I wanted her
The first day we met I allowed myself
to fall in love with my fantasy.

(1,083)

Bounty

My depths
My height
The horizon
Vertical plane
My width
Inner power
A generous gift.
Generosity in giving
(1,084)

Love is Like...

Love is like an obsession
I want you more than anyone else
Love is like a habit
I must see you or I'll have a bad day
Love is like an addiction
if I don't spend time with you, I'll panic,
love is like a fixation
I won't be able to function without you
Love is like a fetish
I need you in my life everyday

(1,085)

Reading Between the Lies

She whispered her love to me
But she kissed another man
She proclaimed her loyalty to me
But told others of my weaknesses
She mentioned I was her best lover
But she moaned another man's name
She called me her best friend
But she spends time with another guy
She told me she loves my favorite meal
But she never cooks it
She told me she'll always be honest with me
But all I hear are lies.

(1,086)

I Promise You

I promise that tomorrow the sun will shine.
I promise that the storm will stop.
I promise that you will laugh again.
I promise that you will love again.
I promise that the hurt will eventually fade.
I promise that the tears will end.
I promise that I'll always be here for you.

(1,087)

Negative Thoughts

How can I get into the habit of writing without
the negative emotions telling me not to?
I can't, the negative emotions will always
be there, I have to write every day no matter how I feel.
I'm not always gonna feel like writing but to achieve
my goals I must keep working.
Just like going to work every day whether I feel like it
or not.
The difference between working at a job and working on my goal is the knowledge of a coming paycheck,
compared to the uncertainty of if or when I'll get
paid for my effort.

(1,088)

Can You Read My Mind

Do you know that thoughts I have of you
Do you know that you make my heart skip a beat
Can you read my mind
Can you see the love in my eyes
Do you feel about me the way I feel about you
Do you want to hold my hand and walk along the shore
Can you read my mind
Can you understand my thoughts
Do you want to wake up next to me
Do you want me to bring you breakfast in bed
Can you read my mind
Are you ready for a love that will last through all time?

(1,089)

Walk Away

I don't want to argue with you
I'm just gonna walk away
I'm not going to explain things to you
I'm just gonna walk away
I'm not gonna fight you
I'm just gonna walk away
I'm not gonna sleep with you
I'm just gonna walk away
I'm not gonna kiss you
I'm just gonna walk away
I'm not gonna love you
I'm just gonna walk away

(1,090)

I Want to be Outside

I work inside
I ride inside the train to get home
I sit in my home watching TV
There isn't any fresh air
There isn't any breeze
Just the A/C blowing freezing stuffy air
I was never claustrophobic
but after these weeks and months
of home and work and back
I'm tired of being inside.
My lungs and my body need fresh air.
We're staying in from the summer heat
Winter is coming and we'll have to stay in
from the cold
I want to be outside breathing the fresh air

(1,091)

Words of Victory

I gave myself a challenge and I accomplished it
I pushed through self-sabotage and self-doubt
I took myself on a journey
and I'm coming to the end
I taught myself to push through and to win
Not to pat myself on the back
but I've found a way to fight
I'm proud of myself for achieving my goal

(1,092)

No Going Back

You will make wrong choices,
but you can't go back
You can make corrections as you go forward
But actions or inactions can't be undone
There is no going back
You said what you felt at the time
You did what you thought was right at the time
You have to accept your actions and move forward
Don't spend time regretting past decisions
move forward trying new decisions

(1,093)

The Mess You Left Behind

In your rage, you mashed my heart
you shattered it to pieces
You scattered my emotions all over the floor
You mixed up my thoughts
I can't think straight
My spirit is bouncing everywhere
banging and slamming into everything
My directions are confused should I
go backward or forward
My mind is in a loop everything is spinning
You left my life a mess
With your accusations and rage

(1,094)

I got da Munchies

My goals have me like a weed head,
I have an appetite that must be fed
Every task I complete gives me a dopamine hit
My goals give me da munchies for my future
Each achievement made, satisfies a desire
a step that was planned
Each completed step
feeds my emotional munchies
Once this goal is finished,
I must set another to feed
the munchies of my mind.

(1,095)

Your Greatest Fear

Is your greatest fear taking a risk to change your life
or living in poverty?
Is your greatest fear living alone
or having no one to love
Is your greatest fear living in the same neighborhood
your whole life or exploring the world
Is your greatest fear eating the same food every day
or trying dishes from around the world
Is your greatest fear not having friends to talk to
or being so boring that no one comes around
Is your greatest fear doing the same job your whole life
or working towards a goal?
Is your greatest fear taking medication every day
or being bedridden
What is your greatest fear

(1,096)

I Wanted

I wanted, years, you gave me months
I wanted love you became a friend
I wanted days you gave me nights
I wanted to be more than a friend,
but friendship was your offer
I wanted to be wanted

(1,097)

This Is Madness

People talk about hating the police,
how they want to murder the police,
and how they want to harm police officers.
But when they have a problem.
They call the police
and expect to be protected.
Make it make sense.

(1,098)

One More

One more day
One more hug
One more chance
One more kiss
One more walk
One more meal
One more song
One more glance
One more time
One more night
One more romance
One more dance
(1,099)

I Write

I don't write about one thing, one topic, one subject,
one time, one situation
I write about everything, the happy times, the sad times,
when I feel motivated, when I feel disillusioned,
I write about it all
Because I've experienced more than one situation
I have more than one emotion
I write about the sunrise. I write about the sunset.
I write about truth, I write about the lies,
I write about my goals.
I write about my dreams. I write about fantasy
I write about my needs, I write about my hopes
I write about who I am and who I want to be.

(1,100)

Closing Words

This is the fourth and final volume of poetry
for the challenge.
It wasn't easy there were a lot of days when I was lost on
what to write. I started to feel drained and tapped out.
Even if it was a Haiku, I expressed myself.
I love writing poetry, short stories,
and my philosophical thoughts.
Thank you, I appreciate your support.
Stone Fauks

Book Titles

A Kaleidoscope of Poetry
1,100 Poem Challenge
vol 1
World on a String
1,100 Poem Challenge
Vol 2
Warm Weather Dance
1,100 Poem Challenge
Vol 3
Victory of Words
1,100 Poem Challenge
Vol 4

www.ingramcontent.com/pod-product-compliance
Lightning Source LLC
Chambersburg PA
CBHW020849090426
42736CB00008B/303

* 9 7 9 8 9 9 1 9 5 4 5 9 4 *